D0766258

Shakespeare on ...
Foreigners

Shakespeare on ...
Foreigners

Katherine and
Elizabeth O'Mahoney

PRION

First published 2002 in Great Britain by
Prion Books Limited
Imperial Works, Perren Street
London NW5 3ED
www.prionbooks.com

Selection copyright © Katherine and
Elizabeth O'Mahoney 2002

ISBN 1-85375-502-8

Cover design by Grade Design Consultants
Printed and bound in Great Britain

Introduction

'The world still consists of two clearly divided groups: the English and the foreigners. One group consists of less than 50 million people; the other of 3,950 million. The latter group does not really count.'

George Mikes

Each summer, French waiters and Spanish barmen are confronted with legions of English tourists, emblazoned from head to toe in Saint George's Cross, demanding a nice cup of tea and a full English breakfast. With our white flabby beer bellies and bald heads festooned with white knotted handkerchiefs, we are proud to be English. Yet, having been invaded by every man and his dog, from the Vikings to the French, we often question what it is to be English. The answer, profound in simplicity and truth, may be found in the plays and poetry of Shakespeare: whatever 'Englishness' might be, it's a damn sight better than being foreign. While the English have always had their problems – social, economic, cultural, intellectual and political – we can always take comfort in the fact we're not French.

This collection of quotations is a testament to the cultural distinctions that make the English 'English' and the other lot 'foreign'. Today, many of us tend to forget that Shakespeare's most famous characters are dodgy foreigners. Time and time again Shakespeare rejects the familiar setting of our green and pleasant isle in favour of far off lands and funny foreigners. Of all his plays only one features an English place name in its short title: *The Merry Wives of Windsor*. Instead, the Bard writes about a merchant in Venice, two gentlemen in Verona, a prince of Denmark, a soldier in Cyprus, twins in Illyria, whole armies in Greece and Rome and an island off the coast of Milan. Scenes from all over the world were recreated on the small stage of the Globe theatre to an audience who never travelled beyond the Mile End Road.

With the Elizabethan stage heaving with such exotic characters, it is hard to believe that Billy Boy never stepped foot on foreign soil. Yet if this is true, where did his fascination grow? Well, Shakespeare would have had to look no further than a London street to find a plethora of foreign faces. Londoners have always been a cosmopolitan people, regardless of the old Anglo-Saxon suspicion of Johnny Foreigner. Like today, Shakespeare's London swarmed with foreign folk, doing business and setting up home. The great Elizabethan capital boasted bulging Belgians, saucy Spaniards, fruity Frenchmen, and others from all over Europe. A constant stream of immigrants flooded into London, driven from their own lands by war, famine and religious persecution until by 1550 it had been claimed that up to half the capital's population was foreign.

Despite their peculiar hygiene habits and indulgence in curious cuisine, this foreign population made an inestimable contribution to English culture. But our ancestors chose to ignore the obvious calibre of our foreign friends, and xenophobia among the English people was rife. Out of fear and ignorance grew farcical myths of strange races and haunted lands, which even penetrated the plays of Shakespeare. In

Othello, the eponymous hero calls to mind that well-known ethnic group whose 'heads do grow beneath their shoulders', while many Elizabethans believed that some exotic races didn't have mouths and survived only on air. Never let it be said, however, that the English were discriminatory in their discrimination; ignorance of different nationalities was generously extended to those closer to home. Indeed, Shakespeare's Londoners reserved their most poisonous bile for the Irish, Welsh and Scots. The intricacies of these national relationships were highly complex: the Irish hated the Scots, the Welsh hated the

Irish, the Scots hated the Welsh and everyone hated the English. The Scots were regarded as being all mouth and no trousers, the Irish were derided for their drunken debauchery, and the Welsh were regarded as ... well ... just a bit silly.

But Shakespeare shows us that while we make gentle jest with our foreign friends, it is these very neighbours who prove crucial in defining England and her people. Shakespeare's history plays confirm that the Elizabethan Englishman is a glorious medley of nationalities: Scandinavian, Roman, French, Irish, Scottish. So while our playful playwright, with a glint in his eye and a smile on his lips, pokes an occasional finger into foreign ribs, Shakespeare's Englishman remains a perfect embodiment of Europe. Therefore, when seeking the essence of 'Englishness' turn not from the Australian youth behind the Soho bar nor from the Lithuanian backpacker asleep on Paddington Station, because it is in foreigners that we find ourselves.

So, showing the spirit that won (and lost) the Empire, let us step forward united in our differences. Let the Frenchman gobble his garlic! Grant the Grecian his lubricated locks! Allow the Belgian to belch his beer! And embrace the foreigners that helped make England great!
Au revoir and toodle-pip!

Katherine and Elizabeth O'Mahoney, 2002

The fig of Spain!

Henry V 3.6.57

Britain is a world by itself.

Cymbeline 3.1.12

Since Frenchmen are so braid,
Marry that will, I live
and die a maid.

All's Well That Ends Well 4.2.74–5

This England never did,
nor never shall,
Lie at the proud feet
of a conqueror.

King John 5.7.112-3

Good Hamlet, cast thy
nighted colour off,
And let thine eye look
like a friend on Denmark.

Hamlet 1 2 68-9

Lord cardinal,
The willing'st sin I
ever yet committed
May be absolved in English.

Henry VIII 3.1.48-50

Eleven of
Shakespeare's plays
are set in Italy,
more than any
other foreign land.

This is the deadly spite
that angers me:
My wife can speak no
English, I no Welsh.

Henry IV Part 1 3.1.189-90

Heavens defend me from that Welsh fairy, lest he transform me to a piece of cheese!

The Merry Wives of Windsor 5.5.80-81

These English woes will
make me smile in France.

Richard III 4.4.115

We think the
subtle-witted French
Conjurers and sorcerers.

Henry VI Part 1 1.1.25-6

Shakespeare wasn't great with foreign names. Foreigners named Antonio appear in *The Merchant of Venice*, *Much Ado About Nothing*, *The Tempest*, *Twelfth Night* and *Two Gentlemen of Verona*.

Foul fiend of France, and hag
of all despite,
Encompass'd with thy lustful
paramours!

Henry VI Part 1 3.5.12-13

Remember where we are:
In France, amongst a fickle
wavering nation.

Henry VI Part 1 4.1.138-9

If the English had
any apprehension, they
would run away.

Henry V 3.7.132

That island of England
breeds very valiant
creatures; their mastiffs
are of unmatchable courage.

Henry V 3.7.137-8

He does smile his face into
more lines than is in the new
map with the
augmentation of the Indies.

Twelfth Night 3.2.74-5

Arm, fight, and conquer,
for fair England's sake!

Richard III 5.5.112

Foreigners were
officially referred to as
'aliens' or 'strangers' in
Elizabethan England.

You will hang like an icicle
on a Dutchman's beard.

Twelfth Night 3.2.26

An old Italian fox
is not so kind.

The Taming of the Shrew 2.1.399

'Tis better using France
than trusting France.

Henry VI Part 3 4.1.41

I reason'd with a
Frenchman yesterday.

The Merchant of Venice 2.8.27

Shakespeare's gravestone originally showed him holding a bag of grain. But in 1747 the people of Stratford replaced the bag with a quill, perhaps in anticipation of the tourists who would come from all over the world to see the monument.

Marry, sir, she's the kitchen
wench and all grease,
and I know not what use to
put her to but to make a
lamp of her and run from her
by her own light. I
warrant, her rags and the
tallow in them will burn a
Poland winter.

The Comedy of Errors 3.2.96-100

Heaven take my soul, and
England keep my bones!

King John 4.3.10

Who is here so vile that
will not love his country?

Julius Caesar 3.2.32

You must not so far prefer
her 'fore ours of Italy.

Cymbeline 1.4.64

Thus, Indian-like,
Religious in mine
error, I adore
The sun, that looks
upon his worshipper,
But knows of him no more.

All's Well That End's Well 2.1.220-3

We'll lay before this
town our royal bones,
Wade to the market-place
in Frenchmen's blood.

King John 2.1.41-2

It has been estimated that foreigners comprised 5 per cent of the population of Elizabethan England.

Pish for thee, Iceland dog!
Thou prick-ear'd cur of Iceland!

Henry V 2.1.39

My affection hath an
unknown bottom, like
the bay of Portugal.

As You Like It 4.1.197-8

We fear not
What can from
Italy annoy us.

Cymbeline 4.3.33-4

Better ten thousand
base-born Cades miscarry
Than you should stoop unto a
Frenchman's mercy.

Henry VI Part 2 4.7.202-3

Now, France, thy glory
droopeth to the dust.

Henry VI Part 1 5.3.29

I seek a wife!
A woman, that is
like a German clock,
Still a-repairing,
ever out of frame,
And never going aright,
being a watch,
But being watch'd that
it may still go right!

Love's Labour's Lost 3.1.184-8

Shakespeare had
seven brothers and
sisters and outlived
them all.

Is this the scourge of France?

Henry VI Part 1 2.3.14

These English monsters!

Henry V 2.2.81

He longs to eat the English.

Henry V 3.7.89

Where is the beauteous
majesty of Denmark?

Hamlet 4.5.21

Come, come, thou art as hot a
Jack in thy mood as
any in Italy, and as soon
moved to be moody, and as
soon moody to be moved.

Romeo and Juliet 3.1.11-3

O noble English that
could entertain
With half their forces
the full pride of France
And let another
half stand laughing by
All out of work,
and cold for action.

Henry V 1.2.110-3

Signior Romeo, bonjour!
There's a French salutation
to your French slop.

Romeo and Juliet 2.3.41-2

Then take my soul,
my body, soul and all,
Before that England
give the French the foil.

Henry VI Part 1 5.3.21-2

Brutus had rather
be a villager
Than to repute himself
a son of Rome.

Julius Caesar 1.2.173-4

My lord, I fear, has
forgot Britain.

Cymbeline 1.6.113

The word 'foreigners' during the Renaissance was generally used to describe English who had abandoned the countryside for London.

It is a recreation to be
by and hear him
mock the Frenchman.

Cymbeline 1.6.77

I would thou didst itch from
head to foot and I had
the scratching of thee – I
would make thee the
loathsomest scab in Greece.

Troilus and Cressida 2.1.28-30

Proud Italy, Whose manners
still our tardy apish nation
Limps after in base imitation.

Richard II 2.1.21-3

You blocks, you stones, you
worse than senseless things!
O you hard hearts, you cruel
men of Rome.

Julius Caesar 1.1 34-5

A woful Cressid 'mongst
the merry Greeks!

Troilus and Cressida 4.5.55

Exceeding pleasant,
none a stranger there
So merry and so gamesome.
He is call'd
The Briton Reveller.

Cymbeline 1.6 60-2

I'll heat his blood with
Greekish wine to-night,
Which with my scimitar I'll
cool to-morrow.

Troilus and Cressida 5.1.1-2

I'll disrobe me
Of these Italian weeds
and suit myself
As does a Briton peasant.

Cymbeline 5.1.22-4

In the 1960s American show *Batman* a bust of Shakespeare is the key that unlocks the batcave.

Sweet honey Greek, tempt me
no more to folly.

Troilus and Cressida 5.2.19

You are dull, Casca,
and those sparks of life
That should be in a Roman
you do want,
Or else you use not.

Julius Caesar 1.3.57-9

There is a Frenchman his
companion, one
An eminent monsieur, that, it
seems, much loves
A Gallian girl at home.
He furnaces
The thick sighs from him,
whiles the jolly Briton –
Your lord, I mean – laughs
from's free lungs.

Cymbeline 1.6.64-8

It is not a fashion for the maids in France to kiss before they are married.

Henry V 5.2.264

I would not be a Roman,
of all nations.

Coriolanus 4.5.179

During the Renaissance,
foreigners with money
could become English by a
royal patent.

Shall not thou and I, between
Saint Denis and Saint
George, compound a boy,
half-French and half-English,
that shall go to
Constantinople and take the
Turk by the beard?

Henry V 5.2.204-7

Cry 'God for Harry! England and Saint George!'

Henry V 3.1.34

I would I were a Roman!

Coriolanus 1.ll.4

Though it appear a
little out of fashion,
There is much care and
valour in this Welshman.

Henry V 4.1.83-4

This paltering
Becomes not Rome.

Coriolanus 3.1.61–2

Something is rotten in
the state of Denmark.

Hamlet 1.4.67

O England! Model to thy
inward greatness
Like little body with a
mighty heart
What might'st thou do, that
honour would thee do,
Were all thy children kind
and natural!

Henry V 2.prologue .15-8

Naught shall make us rue,
If England to itself
do rest but true.

King John 5.7.117-8

Cassio: 'Fore God an excellent song.

Iago: I learned it in England, where indeed they are most potent in potting; your Dane, your German, and your swag-bellied Hollander – drink ho! – are nothing to your English.

Othello 2.3.69-72

The plague of Greece upon
thee, thou mongrel
beef-witted lord!

Troilus and Cressida 2.1.12

Shakespeare's mother, Mary Arden, never lived in the house commonly known as 'Mary Arden's House' in Stratford-Upon-Avon.

O bloody Richard!
Miserable England!

Richard III 3.4.102

I will rather trust a Fleming
with my butter, Parson Hugh
the Welshman with my
cheese, an Irishman with my
aqua-vitae bottle, or a thief to
walk my ambling gelding,
than my wife with herself.

The Merry Wives Of Windsor 2.2.292-6

But when he frown'd, it was against the French
And not against his friends.

Richard II 2.1.179-80

I have heard the Frenchman
hath good skill in his rapier.

The Merry Wives Of Windsor 2.1.208-9

You thought, because he could not speak English in the native garb, he could not therefore handle an English cudgel. You find it otherwise and henceforth let a Welsh correction teach you a good English condition.

Henry V 5.1.71-6

Speak it in French, king:
say, 'pardonne moi.'

Richard II 5.3.117

This royal throne of kings,
this scepter'd isle,
This earth of majesty,
this seat of Mars,
This other Eden, demi-paradise,
This fortress built by
Nature for herself
Against infection and
the hand of war.

Richard II 2.1.40-4

King Phillip: 'Tis France,
for England.

King John: England, for itself.

King John 2.1.202-3

And, like a troop of
jolly huntsmen, come
Our lusty English,
all with purpled hands,
Dyed in the dying
slaughter of their foes.

King John 2.1.321-3

In the May Day riots of 1517 London's foreign community was brutally attacked by angry English workers.

O foul revolt of
French inconstancy!

King John 3.1.248

Fly, noble English, you are bought and sold!

King John 5.4.10

The French fight coldly,
and retire themselves.

King John 5.3.13

Nerissa: How like you the young German, the Duke of Saxony's nephew?

Portia: Very vilely in the morning, when he is sober, and most vilely in the afternoon, when he is drunk. When he is best, he is a little worse than a man, and when he is worst, he is little better than a beast.

The Merchant of Venice 1.2.81-5

Hither return all gilt
with Frenchmen's blood.

King John 2.1.316

Your Italy contains
none so accomplished a
courtier to convince the
honour of my mistress.

Cymbeline 1.4.92-3

I see a yielding in
the looks of France.

King John 2.1.475

Would I had never
trod this English earth,
Or felt the flatteries
that grow upon it!

Henry VIII 3.1.143-4

John Keats, the great Romantic poet, kept a bust of the Bard beside him while he wrote, hoping that Shakespeare would inspire his work.

Is't possible the spells
of France should juggle
Men into such
strange mysteries?

Henry VIII I 3-4

She-wolf of France, but worse
than wolves of France,
Whose tongue more poisons
than the adder's tooth!

Henry VI Part 3 1.4.112-3

What false Italian,
As poisonous-tongued as
handed, hath prevail'd
On thy too ready hearing?

Cymbeline 3.2.4-6

The Frenchmen
are our enemies.

Henry VI Part 2 4.2.167

He can speak French and
therefore he is a traitor!

Henry VI Part 2 4.2.164-5

The Greeks are strong and skilful to their strength, Fierce to their skill and to their fierceness valiant.

Troilus and Cressida 1.1.7-8

She should have stayed in
France and starved
in France.

Henry VI Part 2 1.1.132-3

Assign'd am I to be
the English scourge.

Henry VI Part 1 1.3.108

And how the English
have the suburbs won.

Henry VI Part 1 1.5.2

They call'd us for our
fierceness English dogs.

Henry VI Part 1 1.7.25

Queen Elizabeth I commanded the Lord Mayor 'with great secrecy' to find out 'how many foreigners are residing and remaining within the same, of what nation, profession, trade or occupation every of them are of.'

How the young whelp of
Talbot's, raging-wood,
Did flesh his puny sword in
Frenchmen's blood!

Henry VI Part 1 4.7.35-6

Submission, Dauphin? 'Tis a
mere French word!
We English warriors wot not
what it means.

Henry VI Part 1 4.7.54-5

When I am dead and gone,
Remember to avenge me on
the French.

Henry VI Part 1 1.6.71-2

Mine Italian brain
'Gan in your duller
Britain operate
Most vilely.

Cymbeline 5.6.196-8

That English may as French,
French Englishmen,
Receive each other.
God speak this Amen!

Henry V 5.2.362-3

O fair Katharine, if you will
love me soundly with
your French heart, I will be
glad to hear you
confess it brokenly with your
English tongue.

Henry V 5.2.104-6

This foul Egyptian
hath betrayed me!

Antony and Cleopatra 4.13.10

Now I perceive the
devil understands Welsh.

Henry IV Part 1 3.1.226

A statute of 1483 forbade
foreigners to employ other
foreigners in England.

Lady Percy: Lie still,
ye thief, and hear the lady
sing in Welsh.

Hotspur: I had rather hear
Lady, my brach, howl in Irish.

Henry IV Part 1 3 1 231-3

Cassio: Is your Englishman so expert in his drinking?

Iago: Why, he drinks you, with facility, your Dane dead drunk. He sweats not to over-throw your Almain. He gives your Hollander a vomit, ere the next bottle can be filled.

Othello 2.3.74-8

Pistol: What is thy name?
Henry V: Harry le Roy.
Pistol: Le Roy? A Cornish name!
Art thou of Cornish crew?
Henry V: No, I am
a Welshman.
Pistol: Know'st thou Fluellen?
Henry V: Yes.
Pistol: Tell him, I'll knock his
leek about his pate
Upon Saint Davy's day.

Henry V 4.1.49-56

A sort of vagabonds,
rascals, and runaways,
A scum of Bretons, and
base lackey peasants,
Whom their o'er-cloyed
country vomits forth
To desperate ventures and
assured destruction.

Richard III 5.6.36-9

Let's whip these stragglers
o'er the seas again;
Lash hence these overweening
rags of France.

Richard III 5.6.58-9

If we be conquer'd, let men conquer us,
And not these bastard Bretons, whom our fathers
Have in their own land beat-en, bobb'd, and thump'd,
And in record, left them the heirs of shame.

Richard III 5.6.62-5

O blood-besotted Neapolitan,
Outcast of Naples, England's
bloody scourge!

Henry VI Part 2 5.1.115-6

This happy breed of men,
this little world,
This precious stone set
in the silver sea,
Which serves it in the
office of a wall,
Or as a moat defensive
to a house,
Against the envy of
less happier lands.

Richard II 2.1.45-9

This blessed plot, this earth,
this realm, this England,
This nurse, this teeming
womb of royal kings,
Fear'd by their breed and
famous by their birth,
Renowned for their deeds
as far from home,
For Christian service
and true chivalry,
As is the sepulchre in
stubborn Jewry,
Of the world's ransom,
blessed Mary's Son.

Richard II 2.1.50-6

Antipholus: Where Spain?

Dromio: Faith, I saw it not, but felt it hot in her breath.

The Comedy Of Errors 3.2.133-4

These strong Egyptian
fetters I must break,
Or lose myself in dotage.

Antony and Cleopatra 1.2.108-9

Then, England's ground,
farewell; sweet soil, adieu.
My mother, and my nurse,
that bears me yet!
Where'er I wander,
boast of this I can,
Though banish'd, yet a
trueborn Englishman.

Richard II 1.3.269-72

Shakespeare's play
Cardenio which was
performed in his life, has
been completely lost.

Peace, I say, Gallia and Gaul,
French and Welsh,
soul-curer and body-curer!

The Merry Wives Of Windsor 3.1.89-90

Now I would pray
our 'monsieurs'
To think an English courtier
may be wise,
And never see the Louvre.

Henry VIII 1.3.21-23

For little England
You'd venture an emballing.

Henry VIII 2.3.45-46

I am more an antique
Roman than a Dane.

Hamlet 5.2. 293

Let Rome in Tiber melt.

Antony and Cleopatra 1.1.35

The uncivil kerns of Ireland
are in arms
And temper clay with blood of
Englishmen.

Henry VI Part 2 3.1.310-1

Those girls of Italy,
take heed of them.
They say, our French lack
language to deny,
If they demand, beware
of being captives,
Before you serve.

All's Well That Ends Well 2.1.19-22

Dromio: She is spherical, like a globe. I could find out countries in her.

Antipholus: In what part of her body stands Ireland?

Dromio: Marry sir, in her buttocks. I found it out by the bogs.

The Comedy of Errors 3.2.116-8

Britons strut with courage.

Cymbeline 3.1.33

Woe, woe for England!

Richard III 3.4.80

In Shakespeare's time foreigners were taxed at double the normal rates, were not permitted to own land, and were subject to rigorous work restrictions.

You riband-red nag of Egypt!

Antony and Cleopatra 4.13.10

If we be conquered,
let men conquer us,
And not these bastard Bretons!

Richard III 5.7.62-3

O sweet England!

Othello 2.3.81

O Scotland, Scotland!

Macbeth 4.3.101

The House of Commons passed a bill in 1593 restricting foreign merchants from selling foreign goods.

All the water in Wye cannot
wash your majesty's Welsh
blood out of your body, I can
tell you that.

Henry V 4.8.107

This blessed plot, this earth,
this realm, this England.

Richard II 2.1.50-6

Let Rome in Tiber melt.

Antony and Cleopatra 1.1.35

England we love.

King John 2.1.91

The earliest recorded production of Henry VIII was June 29, 1613, at the Globe Theatre. A cannon used in the production set the thatched roof ablaze and the theatre burned to the ground.